KEEPING PROMISES

WHAT IS SOVEREIGNTY
AND OTHER QUESTIONS ABOUT INDIAN COUNTRY

BY BETTY REID AND BEN WINTON

TUCSON, ARIZONA
WESTERN NATIONAL PARKS ASSOCIATION

Copyright © 2004 by Betty Reid and Ben Winton
Published by Western National Parks Association
The net proceeds from all WNPA publications support educational and research programs in the national parks.
Receive a free Western National Parks Association catalog, featuring hundreds of publications. Email: info@wnpa.org or visit www.wnpa.org

Written by Betty Reid and Ben Winton
Edited by Abby Mogollón
Designed by Melanie Doherty Design
Principal Photography by Gwendolen Cates
Other images: "Portrait of a Man Called Christopher Columbus" by Sebastiano del Piombo, page 6, courtesy The Metropolitan Museum of Art; Mississippi River, page 9, by Charles Gurche; Bosque Redondo, page 13, courtesy National Archives & Records Administration; Gen. George Armstrong Custer, page 13, courtesy National Park Service; Geronimo, page 15, courtesy Arizona Historical Society; Geronimo, page 16, courtesy National Archives & Records Administration; pottery by Maria Martínez, page 17, by Jerry Jacka; Apache woman, page 20, by Chuck Place; boarding school printing office, page 22, courtesy Colorado Historical Society; O'odham basket, page 23, by Chuck Place; boarding school, page 21, courtesy Colorado Historical Society; Code Talkers, page 25, courtesy U.S. Marine Corps; Alcatraz, page 27, Marc Boatwright Alcatraz Collection, courtesy National Park Service; Badlands, page 29, by Tom Till; dancers, page 32, by Chuck Place.

Printing by Sung In
Printed in Korea

INTRODUCTION

A thousand years ago, their names were as diverse as where they lived. They called themselves Chemehuevi, Cocopah, Diné, Duwamish, Guaymi, Hopi, Mi´kmaq, Ojibwa, Pai, Taíno, Yoemem, and more. At least ten million people populated North and South America. In bands, tribes, towns, and cities, these Native peoples celebrated the diversity of cultures through a flourishing trade of art and material goods that extended throughout the Americas.

There was a commonality among all the different peoples, however, in the multitude of different names. When translated, these names carried the essence of saying: We are "The People." We are "human beings."

When Europeans arrived in the Americas more than 500 years ago, they negotiated with these people and recognized their status as inhabitants of the land. These Europeans and, later, American Revolutionists adopted ways of living from these people. In fact, the U.S. system of government is remarkably similar to that of the Iroquois Confederacy in what is now northern New York and southeastern Canada. In the Iroquois Confederacy, representative governments ensured that the will of the people prevailed on major political decisions. Representatives conducted major deliberations in public, giving the community a chance to weigh in. The Iroquois elevated women to the same political and economic status as men. We know that form of governance today as democracy. Such cultural sharing, between Native and non-Native peoples, has slowed considerably in the last 400 years. But it is still happening.

WHAT YOU WILL FIND IN THIS BOOK

You probably want to know the basics: Who is an Indian? What is a tribe? Why do some Native people in the United States live on reservations? And, what is a reservation? Are American Indians citizens of the United States? We'll answer those questions and more.

A QUESTION OF IDENTITY

WHO IS AN INDIAN?

Let's start with the first, and most often asked question: Who is an Indian? When you ask the people most often labeled as such, you get a surprisingly common answer. But the answer is more specific than you might expect.

Adam Teller, a Navajo who lives on the floor of Canyon de Chelly in northeastern Arizona, is a good example. Here, he makes traditional turquoise-and-silver jewelry and greets non-Indian visitors all day, seven days a week. Like most Native people, Teller believes the expression "Indian" fails to describe him. That's a term lawyers, anthropologists, academics, and government officials use. He introduces himself to visitors this way: "I'm Adam Teller and I'm Navajo. It's a [Puebloan] word meaning 'people of the cultivated fields.' But we call ourselves Diné, 'The People.'"

Teller follows the practice of most Indian people, who identify themselves using a word, or words, in their native tongue that describes their cultural grouping. For example, while the English word for one of the Pueblo peoples living in west-central New Mexico is Acoma, this group refers to itself as *Haaku*. Until just fifteen or twenty years ago, "Pima" broadly described a group of Native peoples living in the Sonoran Desert south of Phoenix, Arizona. However, these peoples, who actually are broken into at least four geographic groupings, have always called themselves O'odham (pronounced ought-thumb), which means "The People."

Within the Navajo tribe, Teller introduces himself differently. He first says that he belongs to his mother's clan called *Honaghááhnii*, meaning "People Who Walk Around." Then, he identifies his father's clan. They are *Mahíí Desh Gishnii*, or "Coyote Pass."

Today, a combination of federal laws and the near-extinction of some tribes (while many others were extinguished or merged during the American occupation of tribal lands) often dictate who is legally an "Indian."

According to the U.S. Bureau of Indian Affairs (BIA), the matter is complicated. "No single federal or tribal criterion establishes a person's identity as an Indian," states a BIA publication, in trying to answer the question, "Who is an Indian?"

The answer runs deeper than federal, legal, and even tribal description. It also includes life experience shaped by shared language, stories, and land.

The Northern Cheyenne Reservation covers 445,000 acres in southeastern Montana.

DONALD SANIPASS, JERICH MOREY, MIKMAQ
Gathering ash wood for basket-making, Presque Isle, Maine

THE CONNECTION OF LANGUAGE AND STORIES

In many cultures, not just American Indian ones, the storytelling tradition shapes the view of the universe, thus governing behaviors and the complexities of a society. More than that, this tradition ensures integrity of the culture over many generations. Nowhere is this more evident than among the Native peoples of the Americas. After the European conquest, this tradition has become even more important. LaNada Boyer, a Shoshone-Bannock member of the Fort Hall Indian Reservation in Idaho, put it this way: "We're all just remnants, torn and scattered. Stories [and language] are all we have left."

Native words are packed with power. Native words can heal. Mitchell Blackhorse is a Navajo medicine man from Shiprock, New Mexico, who specializes in a ceremony called the Wind Way. This is a healing ceremony that relies heavily on words—the prayers of the medicine man. Blackhorse is a *haatalii*—a singer trained to cure. When Blackhorse recites a protection prayer, he seeks through his medicine bundle the power of the four sacred mountains that surround traditional Navajo lands to restore a patient. Without the words for that prayer, recited carefully and precisely in his native Navajo, healing fails. So powerful are the words that medicine men have been known to call off a ceremony if they forget the words to a song or prayer, or if they err and do not recite the words in the proper way.

1492

Columbus lands in the Caribbean, though no one today knows exactly where because Columbus's navigation charts suggest he was lost. He claims the Americas for the King of Spain.

THE PEOPLE AND THEIR LAND

Tribes often define their land area by sacred mountains, by rivers, and by other natural resources that hold both spiritual significance and economic importance, such as for food and trade items.

For example, to the Acoma people, the juniper-dotted high desert of New Mexico is more than a place where they have resided since this world was created. It is the place where they will *always* live, and they must care for it so it will sustain them.

El Malpais National Monument, New Mexico

Haaku is the name they use to describe themselves. It is an ancient word that means "to prepare" a place where the people can live and practice their culture freely. More specifically, *Haaku* includes the lava fields in El Malpais National Monument. It is a sacred space, says Brian Vallo, a member of the Acoma Pueblo and director of the pueblo's Acoma Tourist Center. Vallo hopes that park visitors realize that the ground on which they walk is inextricably tied to the spiritual well-being of the Acoma, and it must always be preserved in order to the ensure the harmony and health of the people.

1680

In August, the northern pueblos of New Mexico join together in the Pueblo Revolt, expelling the Spaniards from the area for the next twelve years.

CAMILLE LACAPA,
LAC COURTE OREILLES OJIBWE/HOPI/TEWA
General Manager of WOJB-FM Radio, one of more than thirty-five Native-run radio stations in the U.S., Hayward, Wisconsin

Crow Fair encampment on
Little Big Horn River, Montana

"When Pueblo people come to the table to discuss land, water, and other natural resource issues, we don't begin with talking about what's before us today. Rather, we start with our creation and that of the world. We were given this responsibility to protect and use resources as they were intended for us, and they were not to be destroyed or desecrated, but to be honored and protected," Vallo says.

What the Acoma and other Pueblo peoples did on their own for thousands of years now takes place largely under the direction and control of the federal government. Places the Pueblo peoples consider sacred are now contained within the boundaries of national parks such as El Morro National Monument, Bandelier National Monument, and Petroglyph National Monument.

On the latter, the Acoma find themselves squeezed between two governments—the city of Albuquerque, which proposed building a highway that could threaten to erase some of the rock art revered by the tribe as containing important religious information, and the federal government, which controls access to their cultural property on parklands.

Vallo describes the situation as nothing short of a battle to protect what is most sacred to the Acoma.

In spite of such a battle, he finds hope in the visitors who come to these parks. Most, he says, have a genuine interest in learning more about the Native peoples of

1830

Congress passes the Indian Removal Act mandating removal of many American Indians from east of the Mississippi River to Indian Territory in Oklahoma.

1832–32

The Cherokee sue the state of Georgia for the right to stay on their lands. In *Cherokee Nation v. Georgia* (1831) and *Worcester v. Georgia* (1832), the U.S. Supreme Court upholds the Cherokee people's right to stay on their lands.

the area. Most, he also says, want to show respect for those natural resources that the original inhabitants consider to be culturally important.

HOW MANY INDIANS LIVE IN THE UNITED STATES?

Because the definitions of who is an Indian can vary widely, the subsequent question of how many Indians exist in the United States today is also quite vague. The Bureau of the Census, which counts anyone as Indian who says they are Indian, counted 1,959,234 such people in the 2000 census. The Bureau of Indian Affairs maintains a more conservative estimate of those who are likely to be "real" Indians. In 1993, about 1.2 million people were American Indian or Alaska Native, according to the BIA. (If you apply the Census Bureau's 37.9 percent growth rate since 1993, that would mean that approximately 1.6 million people today qualify under federal standards as being American Indian.)

But you cannot answer the question "how many" without also looking at who is included in the term "Indian." The BIA uses the term "American Indian" along with "Alaska Native," "Eskimo," and "Aleut" to broadly describe all Native peoples. There are the Native Hawaiians, as well. Then, we also see the term "Native American" floating around.

The BIA says "Native American" is outdated. It stopped using it in the 1960s after some Indian groups protested that it failed to describe them as the first

1831–1837
Trail of Tears
Federal troops force Choctaw, Chickasaw, Creek,
Cherokee, and Seminole to walk to Oklahoma,
many during frigid winter weather.

KAITLYN STEVENS, TLINGIT
Klukwan, Alaska

people of this hemisphere. After all, most Americans born here are "native," or so the argument goes.

The Eskimos and Aleuts in Alaska are two culturally distinct groups and are sensitive about being included under the "Indian" designation. They prefer "Alaska Native."

Given all this, Native people say it's best just to refer to them in the same way that they refer to themselves—by their tribal name. So, call a Hopi a Hopi, not a Native American. Call a member of the Tohono O'odham Nation a Tohono O'odham, not an American Indian.

But what do you do if there is a broad class of many different tribal groups that you want to refer to generically? That verdict is still out, but many wordsmiths and cultural experts have begun using the term "Native people" or "Natives," with a capital N. The Associated Press Stylebook, which is commonly used for mass media writing, in an effort to make things clear rather than push a political agenda, has this bit of wisdom: " 'American Indian' is the preferred term for those in the United States. Where possible, be precise and use the name of the tribe: He is a Navajo commissioner...."

HOW DO INDIANS DETERMINE WHOM THEY ALLOW IN THE TRIBE?

Native people of what is now the United States have accepted the term "Indian"

1838

Ignoring the U.S. Supreme Court, President Jackson sends federal troops to forcibly remove Cherokee people.

as their own and use it universally to describe anyone who shares their language, worldview, and bloodline.

Oftentimes, you will hear American Indian people say that they are an "enrolled member" of such-and-such tribe. Tribes decide, in most cases by bloodline, who will be a member.

It's important to understand how tribes view bloodlines. In the strictest cultural sense, many American Indian tribes have a matrilineal and, less often, a patrilineal system, in which nearly anyone born into the tribe is considered a member of the tribe. Some tribes have a bilineal system as well. The European-American distinctions of cousin, brother, sister, aunt, uncle, and so on don't exist in the same fashion. Many tribes define bloodline relationships based on the matrilineal system. Here is one example: In Indian Country, what non-Indians might call a maternal uncle would be a "father" to his nieces and nephews. His responsibility is to help ensure that the children grow up properly and have a good life. Of course, the biological father also shares that responsibility. But the old African adage, "It takes a village to raise a child," is equally true for many American Indian cultures.

In some tribes, those who marry into the tribe also are considered members, but in the sense that they are obligated to uphold tribal laws and traditions and support their spouse and the spouse's relatives. Non-Indian in-laws do not get the

Riders on the Chief Big Foot Memorial Ride, which memorializes the massacre at Wounded Knee in 1890.

right to be enrolled in the tribe by virtue of marriage. However, the children of such marriages may qualify for enrollment.

For federally recognized tribes, enrollment is important. Ultimately, the U.S. government—at least in the last 100 years—has resorted to letting these tribes—there are some 558 as of this writing—decide who should be an enrolled member.

For each tribe, membership requirements are different. For example, to be enrolled in the Navajo Nation as a tribal member, one must be at least one-quarter Navajo. In the Pascua Yaqui Nation, where the tribe closed enrollment in the 1980s, enrollment has been more stringent—at least one-quarter Pascua Yaqui and you must be the direct lineal descendant of an enrolled member. Hence, one could be full-blooded Pascua Yaqui and still not be eligible for enrollment if his or her mother or father or grandparents never enrolled in the tribe.

For tribes, such as the Houma of Louisiana, that do not yet have U.S. recognition,

1848

U.S. wins the U.S.-Mexican War and purchases territory, which becomes the states of California, Utah, Nevada, Arizona, New Mexico, and Colorado, from Mexico for $5,000,000. Native peoples in this area now fall under U.S. jurisdiction for the first time. Some tribes along the newly formed border are divided. Today, a portion of the Tohono O'odham tribe remains on the Mexico side of the border, caught in an international jurisdictional quandary.

1851

The U.S. Army establishes Fort Defiance near present-day Window Rock, Arizona. Already tense relations erupt into violence between the military and the Navajo.

The Crow Fair is a time for Native people to come together.

membership is often determined through a complex combination of historical documentation, such as birth records and other official records, and the tribe's own cultural standards. But because the U.S. government refuses to recognize the Houma, this tribe does not have land set aside for its use and does not receive any federally subsidized medical care or other funding.

WHAT IS A TRIBE?

Originally, a "tribe" was a body of people bound together by blood ties who were socially, politically, and religiously organized; who lived together in a defined territory; and who spoke a common language or dialect.

Today, the federal government uses "tribe" to define a body or group of people it officially recognizes as having a legitimate, ancestral claim to land based on established language and cultural practices. The government criteria are complex and sometimes disputed mixtures of anthropological and legal definitions. As a result, the criteria can often fail to fully acknowledge Native cultures that remain alive today. For example, the Mashpee Wampanoag tribe in southeastern Massachusetts, which is well-known to the people of New England as a legitimate tribe, still fails to meet U.S. criteria for federal recognition because it cannot produce all the detailed historical documentation that the government requires.

1863

Colonel Christopher "Kit" Carson forces Navajo leaders to surrender. U.S. troops force the Diné (Navajo people) to walk "The Long Walk," some 350 miles east, from what is now Window Rock, Arizona, to Bosque Redondo (Fort Sumner) in New Mexico.

The Crow Fair,
Crow Agency, Montana

Similarly, many who have lived in the Southeast for generations recognize the Houma people of Louisiana as a legitimate tribal entity. But the Houma also fail to meet the stringent federal definitions to win formal acknowledgement.

To tribes that succeed in winning federal recognition, the U.S. government provides enrolled tribal members health care services and some educational opportunities. Tribes receive land and—most important—the right, to some extent, to govern themselves—the right to sovereignty.

WHAT IS A SOVEREIGNTY?

"Sovereignty" has been a touchy and much debated topic in Indian Country. Legally, according to American Indian scholars, sovereignty means the power to self-govern. This means the tribal government's ability to collect funds to finance programs or develop enterprises on their land.

Sovereignty means a charter of freedom to be Indian, says attorney Raymond Cross, a Mandan/Hidatsa member who works at the University of Montana. He adds that it is the right to speak the language, a right to protect the environment, and a right to pursue justice on the reservation as well as for tribal members.

Rebecca Tsosie, Pascua Yaqui and executive director of the Indian Legal Institute at Arizona State University, includes another element to the definition

1866

The United States assigns the Navajo Reservation land and allows imprisoned Navajo to return home from Bosque Redondo on foot.

1876

On June 25, Gen. George Armstrong Custer and his solders are killed when they attack a large hunting camp of Arapaho, Blackfoot, Brule, Cheyenne, Hunkpapa, Oglala, Sans Arc, and Miniconjou on Montana's Little Bighorn River.

of sovereignty. It is one of the most important features of what nationhood is all about, she says. That element is something called political autonomy, in other words, the right for American Indians to debate and decide their future on their own, without outside oversight or interference. "It's what Indian nations always had been before the federal government came along," she says. "A lot of people think of it as a governmental power. It has to mean the ability to determine the whole essence of the group."

But the right to self-government comes with a price.

THE RESERVATION SYSTEM

LAND HELD IN RESERVE

Among the heftiest prices to pay for sovereignty revolves around the land. Originally, an "Indian reservation" was land reserved by the U.S. government for a tribe that relinquished some or all of its traditional lands to the U.S. government. More recently, congressional acts, executive orders, and administrative rulings have created reservations. The U.S. government often sets aside these tracts of land for tribes it recognizes, giving tribes the right to occupy and govern themselves on the land. The U.S. government

LONNIE FRITZLER, CROW
Crow Reservation, Lodge Grass, Montana

holds the land in trust, or reserve, for the tribes, meaning that tribes cannot sell or trade the land. The federal government can also hold non-reservation land in trust for the benefit of tribes. Examples include oil- or mineral-rich land that can be leased, with the revenues going to the tribe or to tribal members.

THE MEANING OF "TRUST"

So if tribes do have a certain sense of being sovereign, the logical question remains: Why does the U.S. government hold Native lands in "trust" and maintain what it calls a "trust relationship" with these "nations"?

Technically, the Bureau of Indian Affairs has this explanation as of this writing: "Nearly all lands of Indian Tribes…are held in trust for them by the United States. There is no general law that permits a tribe to sell its land. Individual Indians also own trust land, which they can sell, but only upon the approval of the Secretary of the Interior or his representative. If an Indian wants to extinguish the trust title to his land and hold title like any other citizen (with all the attendant responsibilities such as paying taxes), he can do so if the Secretary of the Interior or his authorized representative determines that he is able to manage his own affairs. This is a protection for the individual."

Indian lawyers have a slightly different way of framing the trust relationship. Many tribes, says Rebecca Tsosie, have set up their own systems for parceling out reservation land to families that have a family or religious claim to certain areas. One system, for example, is the "homesite lease," in which the tribe will allow members to occupy parcels within the reservation for building homes, for operating businesses, and for agricultural purposes on a leased basis.

HOW MANY RESERVATIONS ARE THERE?

There are approximately 275 Indian land areas that the United States administers as Indian reservations. Reservations can range in size from very small—just a few acres—to extremely large. Their size and shape are sometimes arbitrarily determined and other times follow natural landforms and religious boundaries recognized by the tribe.

The largest reservation, in terms of land size, is the Navajo Nation, with a land mass roughly equal to that of West Virginia. In Alaska, Native land areas are divided into "corporations," which in some cases cover areas roughly one-third the size of Texas. The Tohono O'odham Nation along the Arizona-Mexico border has four separate reservation tracts that add up to 2.8 million acres—roughly the size of Connecticut. Many of the smaller reservations are less than 1,000 acres, with the smallest being less than 100 acres. On each reservation, the local governing authority is the tribal government.

1886

Geronimo and his band of Chiricahua Apache warriors surrender after more than two decades of armed conflict with the U.S. government. Geronimo and his band (including women and children) are sent by train to Florida and imprisoned at St. Augustine, a Spanish-colonial-era fortress.

1887

Congress passes the General Allotment Act of 1887, which allows the government to sell "surplus" Indian lands to non-Indian homesteaders.

The Secretary of the Interior serves as trustee of this land, in accordance with a 1876 congressional act, and later laws and regulations, which dictate that the land will be preserved for the use of the Native people for whom it was reserved. Combined, about 56.2 million acres of land are held in trust by the United States for various tribes and American Indian individuals.

The states in which reservations are located have limited powers over the land, and only as provided by federal law.

CAN ANYONE·BUY AND SELL RESERVATION LAND?

Because this land is held in trust by the federal government for the exclusive use of federally recognized tribes, even the members of the tribes themselves cannot purchase or sell land within the reservation's boundaries. So that people have a secure right to use a piece of land for a certain length of time, some tribal governments arrange homesite leases. Other tribes use more traditional ways to divide up the land, such as by clan system or historical occupation of specific areas.

WHO LIVES ON RESERVATION LAND?

Who gets to live on reservation land? Indians, of course. Many non-Indians also live on reservation land, either because their jobs require it, or because they are married to a tribal member. Sometimes tribes hire people with special skills, such as environmental experts, teachers, doctors, lawyers, or engineers, to help the tribe develop. These individuals are allowed to rent homes or lease a plot of land on the reservation, but they can never own the land.

Since 1924, American Indians are American citizens. So they have the same rights as all other citizens to buy and sell land elsewhere—so long as it is not trust land—and to live wherever they want, either on the reservation or off.

Largely for economic reasons—unemployment hovers near 50 percent on most reservations—the vast majority of Native peoples live off the reservation. But each weekend look for a steady stream of cars and trucks flowing toward the reservation as people head home to visit relatives, attend special events such as fairs, and participate in traditional religious observances tied to ancestral land bases.

1898
Congress passes the Curtis Act, which mandates allotment of tribal lands in Indian Territory (Oklahoma) and ends tribal sovereignty in the area.

1904
Geronimo exhibited along with other Native peoples at the St. Louis World's Fair.

RESERVATIONS IN THE UNITED STATES

There are approximately 275 land areas administered as reservations in the U.S.
Map Source: The U.S. Census Bureau.

1919

Maria and Julian Martinez, of San Ildefonso
Pueblo in New Mexico, begin making a distinctive
glossy black pottery, which marks the start of the
market for Native arts and crafts.

BETWEEN NATIONS

In fall 1958, a non-Indian trader working on the Navajo Reservation wanted to collect a debt from a Navajo customer. The trader took the Navajo to state court. The issue was obvious: The customer owed money to the trader.

Nonetheless, the trader lost when it was heard by the U.S. Supreme Court. Arizona lacked jurisdiction, said Justice Hugo Black, over a matter involving an American Indian on tribal lands.

Black wrote, "There can be no doubt that to allow the exercise of state jurisdiction here would undermine the authority of the tribal courts over Reservation affairs, and hence would infringe on the right of the Indians to govern themselves. It is immaterial that respondent is not an Indian. He was on the Reservation, and the transaction with an Indian took place there."

The case is called *Williams v. Lee*, 358 U.S. 217 (1959). It helped set the stage for the actions surrounding tribal sovereignty.

"This victory reserved the right for Navajos to regulate their own affairs free from state interference," says historian and author Peter Iverson, who has spent a lifetime researching Native social and political issues. He says that U.S. courts are beginning to recognize what the federal government did not for centuries: American Indian tribes have sovereign rights—above and beyond those of cities, towns, and counties within America.

In more than 300 years of deal-making between Native peoples and Anglo-Europeans this kind of case may seem like just another blip on the historical timeline. It isn't. The case illustrates the ongoing legal and political sentiment in modern America that tribes are sovereign and ought to be dealt with accordingly.

In the beginning, every tribe in North America had its own system of government built along social, political, religious, and cultural frameworks. Some of those systems were not unlike the current democratic form of U.S. government. Indeed, much of the original system of U.S. democracy is similar to that of eastern woodlands tribes, such as the Iroquois, who used a representative form of open government that sought to ensure that every voice in the community participated in important decisions.

Chief Big Foot Memorial Ride, Pine Ridge
Reservation, Badlands, South Dakota

If a dispute occurred, many North American Indian tribes built consensus to resolve matters. In some tribes, it was the women who had the final say on issues. That is because many tribes are matrilineal, which ensured that not only bloodlines but also property passed from the mother's family.

In governmental decision-making, men made the recommendations and often held titles, such as "head man" or "chief," and their proposals and plans were hashed out with the concerns and issues of the community in mind.

As Euro-American influences began to overtake tribal systems of governance, all that began to change.

British, French, and Spanish colonial influences divided tribes, who sided with one European group or another in order to try to retain their original lands and cultures. Political acculturation began to occur, and the more powerful European newcomers often did not recognize the traditional ways of governance.

Between the 1700s and early 1900s, the dominant European and then U.S. government outlawed many systems of government, and tribes were relocated off their traditional lands. This effectively broke down the sovereign, intertribal governmental relationships that had existed between tribes for centuries.

HOW THE IDEA OF TREATIES DEVELOPED

Since the 1500s, Europeans and the original inhabitants of the Western Hemisphere have negotiated some 1,000 "agreements," or treaties. Spaniards issued decrees claiming land on behalf of the king and promising to bring God and civilization to the Natives. Fur traders made deals with tribes in the Great Lakes region to gain access to the land for hunting and to set prices for pelts collected by the Native peoples. Later, in the early eighteenth century, the French and British made deals with tribes for access to land, hunting, and fishing rights. After the French ceded all land east of the Mississippi, the British colonists began pushing west, despite the Royal Proclamation of 1763 that forbade settlement west of the Appalachians.

Treaty-making was part of the American government's Revolutionary War strategy. Treaties were intended to prevent tribes from siding with the British.

The U.S. precedent of treating tribes as sovereign nations goes back to its first treaties. In 1778, the Continental Congress made a deal with the Delaware people. This tribe had migrated from its traditional lands along the Delaware River into what is now Ohio and western Pennsylvania after European settlers had encroached on their lands. In return for a military alliance, Congress said it would accept a new state if the tribe formed its own and entered into the newly created United States.

1921

U.S. Bureau of Indian Affairs issues a circular known as the "Short Hair Order," which orders men to cut their hair and suppresses "immoral" tribal dances.

1922

The Gallup Intertribal Ceremonial provides an annual gathering for American Indians to exhibit their tribal dances, art, and other aspects of culture.

1922

The Santa Fe Indian Market is founded, providing a world-renowned market for Native artwork.

Treaty-making with foreign nations was always a federal prerogative in order to ensure consistency in nation-to-nation relationships and prevent conflicting agreements from occurring. This reasoning worked with treaties with American Indians, too. By 1830, Congress outlawed treaties between states and tribes, thus imposing federal control over the agreement process. In spite of that, partly because of political and economic pressures from a land-hungry nation, Congress failed to ratify many of the federal treaties with tribes. Indeed, some 600 treaties or agreements have either been broken or never ratified, according to the Native American Rights Fund and other legal scholars. Some 370 other treaties were approved.

WHEN INDIANS BECAME WARDS OF THE GOVERNMENT

Ultimately, Congress ended its policy of treaty-making in 1871 and instead declared that American Indians were "wards" of the federal government, who would be better served if they were assimilated into American society. The government set up formal "reservations," or reserves of land, for tribes that it chose to recognize. Today, some 558 tribes are recognized by the U.S. government as "legitimate," based on political, historical, and anthropological criteria, and not all of them have reservation land. Many other tribes that were either assimilated or dispersed have legitimate cultural and bloodline claims to authenticity but do not meet the strict

1924
Congress makes all American Indians U.S. citizens, entitling Native people to the right to vote in national elections.

1934
Congress passes the Indian Reorganization Act, which in part encourages American Indians to "recover" their cultural heritage. It allows government-run Indian schools to teach art and ends the General Allotment Act of 1887. In order to take advantage of funding under the IRA, tribes are required to adopt a U.S.-style constitution. While many tribes do adopt a constitution, many others refuse.

U.S. government criteria that would qualify them to operate their own government.

It would be nearly a century after treaty-making ended before the prevailing principle behind such agreements—that tribes are sovereign nations—was embraced again.

WINNING BACK SOVEREIGNTY

Nineteenth- and twentieth-century efforts to remove Indian lands and to assimilate Native peoples into American life had the unexpected effect of also paving the way for tribes to win back sovereignty.

EDUCATION AND RESERVATIONS

Education became key to the fight. At first, education was achieved by forcibly sending children to boarding schools far from home, where disciplinarians tried to stamp out the "Indian" in American Indians and turn them into dark-skinned proto-European copies of the settlers who had "founded" America. The methodology was derived from a U.S. Army captain's nineteenth-century motto "kill the Indian, save the man." Indian boarding schools carried a military air about their routines, where children scrubbed toilets with toothbrushes, lived in barracks-style dormitories, and marched in military drills.

Several other nineteenth-century events helped foreshadow modern sovereignty

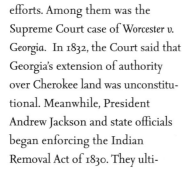

Miccosukee Preschoolers, Miccosukee
Reservation, Tamiami Trail, Florida

RUSS LENO, GRAND RONDE
World War II veteran, Grand Ronde Reservation, Oregon

efforts. Among them was the
Supreme Court case of Worcester v.
Georgia. In 1832, the Court said that
Georgia's extension of authority
over Cherokee land was unconstitu-
tional. Meanwhile, President
Andrew Jackson and state officials
began enforcing the Indian
Removal Act of 1830. They ulti-
mately forced thousands of Choctaw, Chickasaw, Creek, and Seminole to move to
what is now Oklahoma, in many cases by walking. Many people died during these
winter walks, known as the Trail of Tears. Once there, they were forced to live on
land given to them by the federal government. In 1838 the Cherokee met the same
fate, as Georgia officials simply refused to honor the Court opinion. But the
Supreme Court opinion would set precedent extending into the twentieth century.

By 1924, American Indians had won the right to become U.S. citizens. Once
again, education entered the picture: The government forced the children of these
new citizens to attend schools—boarding schools much like the ones of the
nineteenth century. But out of those oppressive, federally funded, boarding school

1935

The Indian Arts and Crafts Board is created.
The board encourages Native arts and crafts
by funding art classes and placing a trademark
on products guaranteeing that "real" Indians
have produced them.

late 1930s

U.S. Bureau of Indian Affairs begins closing boarding
schools and allows children to attend schools in
their home communities. Despite this new policy,
boarding schools continue to forcibly remove children
from families into the mid-1960s.

environments, a few American Indians became doctors, educators, and, most important when it comes to sovereignty issues, lawyers.

INDIAN REORGANIZATION PERIOD

The year 1932 marked a critical turning point in American Indian governance. President Franklin Roosevelt appointed John Collier Commissioner of Indian Affairs. Collier, knowledgeable about and respectful of Native cultures, wanted to reverse previous policies hostile to traditional cultural practices.

Collier brought economic improvements to the reservations, including many of Roosevelt's New Deal programs intended to counteract the negative effects of the Great Depression. He created the Indian Civilian Conservation Corps to boost employment, and he established the Indian Arts and Crafts Board to promote sales of goods made by American Indians. He also sought to end the government's policy of banning Indian religious ceremonies, as well as to stop the sale of lands allotted to tribes.

However, the most sweeping change during this period was the passage of the Indian Reorganization Act of 1934, which gave tribes the power to govern themselves and control their lands. Both Indians and non-Indians opposed the original version, which contained revolutionary proposals, but eventually it allowed tribes to

VINCENT KITCHEYAN, JR., HO-CHUNK/APACHE
PRESTON E. TONEPAHHOTE, JR., KIOWA/MAYAN
WALTER GEORGE STONEFISH WILLIS, OJIBWE/DELAWARE
LARENIA FELIX, DINÉ
KEVIN TARRANT, HOPI/HO-CHUNK
LANCE RICHMOND, MOHAWK
Silvercloud Singers, New York City

adopt constitutions, many of which are modeled after the U.S. Constitution, and to establish tribal councils.

By the 1950s, the U.S. government again shifted policy and imposed "termination" in order to wipe out the federal recognition of tribes—and, therefore, services provided by the U.S. government. The policy did not last long enough to eliminate all tribes but did wipe out more than sixty federally recognized groups. At the same time, a small pool of American Indian attorneys was forming. They began to re-examine laws and public policy regarding the status of the American Indian.

THE EVOLUTION OF INDIAN POLITICAL ACTIVISM

Wayne Chattin, a member of the Blackfeet Nation, remembers how it all began in the 1950s. Chattin had just graduated from the University of Montana and was anxious to help Indian people. He saw only a handful of college-educated Indian people. "I could count on one hand the number of Indian lawyers," he says. "Yet, there were these issues—natural resources, economic development, and health care."

Because there were so few Indian lawyers, and even fewer tribal dollars to hire them, these early "political pioneers" went to work in the federal government, in places such as the Office of Economic Opportunity and the Economic Development Administration. They quietly began using their influence as government offi-

Activists bring Native issues to the political forefront.

1940s

Code Talkers help the U.S. win World War II battles in the South Pacific by using their Native languages. Tribes include the Comanche, Hopi, and the Navajo.

1953

A series of federal laws called the Termination Acts wipe out more than sixty tribes. Termination policy includes settling all federal obligations to a tribe, withdrawing federal support (for example health services and education), and closing the reservation. Frequently, tribal members are then relocated to urban areas. Affected tribes include the Klamaths, the Paiutes, the Poncas, and the Catawbas.

BIRGIL KILLS STRAIGHT, OGLALA LAKOTA

Traditionalist, author, former educator, programs administrator, founder of the Chief Big Foot Memorial Ride, Pine Ridge Reservation, South Dakota

Women's Canoe-Racing Team, Quinault Reservation, Taholah, Washington

1961

More than 500 people gather for the American Indian Chicago Conference to promote tribal sovereignty and survival. Later that year, a more activist organization called the National Indian Youth Council is formed. Many other Indian organizations are formed throughout the 1960s, seeking to end termination and relocation policies and demanding self-determination for Indian peoples.

cials to benefit tribes. By the early 1970s, Chattin had joined them, serving as director of Native American programs for the Bicentennial administration. Later, in the Department of the Interior he served in a senior position in the BIA's Office of Self-Determination and then as a senior staff assistant to the assistant secretary of Indian affairs. Chattin was representative of many American Indians who chose to work inside the system to create change.

Meanwhile, the University of New Mexico Law School in Albuquerque became a mecca for young American Indians seeking to change the system by becoming lawyers. The federal government's policy of terminating the status of tribes, the lack of jobs, and America's movement into the 1960s era of activism only egged on these bright minds, says Sam Deloria, the dean of the American Indian law program at UNM.

Kirk Kickingbird, president of the Native American Bar Association in Oklahoma City, describes it this way: "We felt like Bronze Age warriors given the gift of a Damascus steel blade. No enemy could stand before us. We shared [Sam] Deloria's cynical humor when he twisted the Civil Rights Movement's anthem of 'We shall overcome,' into 'We shall overrun.'

"And when our friends took the anthem too literally [such as the 1972 armed takeover and shootout with FBI agents at Wounded Knee, S.D.] lawyers were needed more than ever," Kickingbird said.

TONY BISSONETTE, MERVIN GARNEAUX, ALBERT AMERICAN HORSE, VINCENT TEN FINGERS, OGLALA LAKOTA
Veterans Powwow, Pine Ridge Reservation, South Dakota

1969
Dennis Banks and George Mitchell, two Chippewa (Anishinaabe) living in Minneapolis–St. Paul, organize the American Indian Movement (AIM) to protest police brutality against Indians.

1969
Eighteen-month occupation of the abandoned island of Alcatraz in San Francisco Bay begins. The occupation brings national attention to problems in Indian Country and results in federal legislation that improves education funding, the return of sacred lands, and more.

JOHN TRUDELL
SANTEE SIOUX
Poet, recording artist,
national spokesman during
the 1969-71 Indians of All
Tribes Occupation of
Alcatraz Island,
National Chairman of the
American Indian
Movement from 1973 to
1979, Los Angeles,
California

JIM NORTHRUP, ANISHINAABE
Author, poet, storyteller, Vietnam veteran with his grandson
AARON DOW, ANISHINAABE
Sawyer, Minnesota

Law, it seemed even then, would be what shaped and defined "sovereignty" for tribes. But what tribes still lacked was political clout. For that, tribes needed money. They were beyond broke. Census statistics painted Indian Country as bleak—with people living in Third World conditions. The prospect of hiring lobbyists or other political experts to influence Washington, D.C., was nearly impossible for many tribes.

So, American Indians found other ways to be heard in the 1960s and 1970s. One of the most famous was the occupation by a small band of American Indian intellectuals, artists, educators, and activists in November 1969 of Alcatraz Island in San Francisco Bay. They took over the abandoned federal prison and held it for more than a year and a half, issuing a number of demands ranging from increased educational opportunities to the return of sacred lands taken by the federal government. While some of their demands were met, their most important accomplishments included bringing to the forefront that American Indian people not only had the same rights as all other Americans to be heard, but the era of their simply behaving as if they were "wards of the government" had ended.

1970
President Richard Nixon formally ends the Termination Policy.
The Sacred Blue Lake, in the Sangre de Cristo Mountains,
and 48,000 surrounding acres are returned to Taos Pueblo.
The Pueblo consider the lake vital to their religion. In 1904,
the United States had made the lake area a national forest
and restricted the Pueblo's access to the region.

FRANCES MANUEL, TOHONO O'ODHAM
Basket maker, authority on indigenous plants
Tohono O'odham Nation, San Pedro Village, Arizona

After Alcatraz, the government began to pay attention. It quietly ended the policy of terminating tribal recognition, returned several thousand acres of land to tribes, and recommitted to working with tribes on a government-to-government basis.

At about the same time, the first wave of federal lawsuits filed by Indian attorneys began to appear. Throughout the 1980s, tribes saw numerous legal victories, ranging from winning federal recognition to financial reparations to cleanup of illegal toxic wastes on their lands.

Some nations developed their own Departments of Justice. These new departments were staffed with American Indian and non-Indian attorneys who were eager to win more sovereign rights for tribes.

Thanks to these efforts, Indian political influence, gained largely by the use of the legal system and new economic clout, is much different than in the last two centuries. Some tribes are starting to see new revenue sources from economic development and gaming. New wealth often means that tribes can hire more, and better, lawyers. It means they can educate their members. They can hire lobbyists. Doors once closed to them in Washington are now open. And it means they can create even more economic opportunities in order to truly be self-governing, or, in other words, sovereign.

1973

AIM and Lakota Sioux tribal members occupy the trading post at Wounded Knee Village to draw attention to problems on the Pine Ridge Reservation in South Dakota.

1975

Congress passes the Indian Self-Determination Act in response to the storm of Indian protests. The act states in part that "the Congress hereby recognizes the obligation of the United States to respond to the strong expression of the Indian people for self-determination by assuring maximum Indian participation in the direction of educational as well as other Federal services to Indian communities so as to render such services more responsive to the needs and desires of those communities."

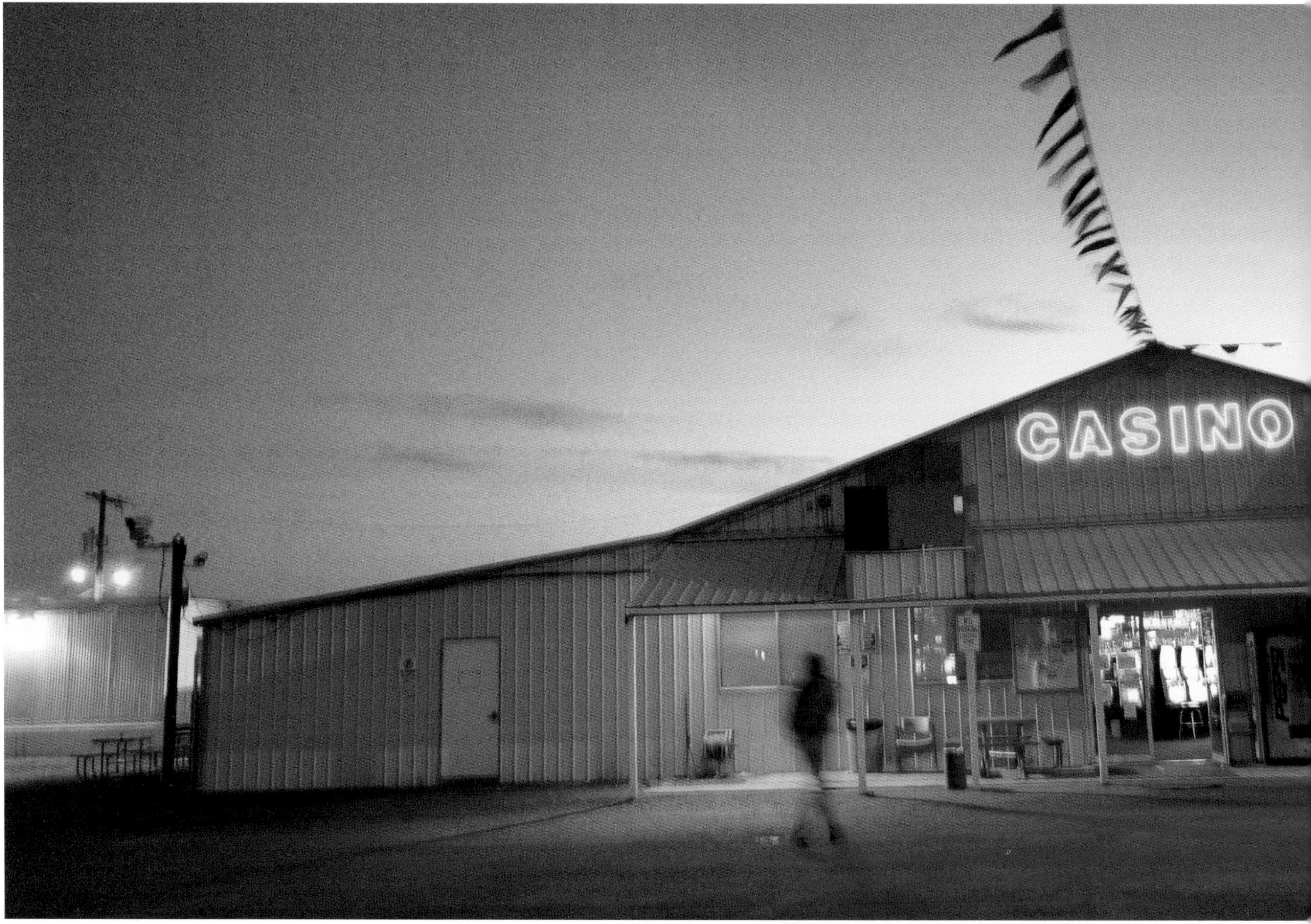
CASINO

BEYOND CULTURAL SURVIVAL:
NATIONAL AND LOCAL AFFAIRS

The issue of sovereignty is more than one of cultural survival. It is also economically and politically charged. American Indian politicians use the topic to try to leverage negotiations with state and federal governments. Tribal members use it to claim rights to land and exemptions from taxation and civil and criminal prosecution. Businessmen use the term to help shape relationships that might give them an advantage in doing business on a reservation. The legal and historical framework around sovereignty is complex and often muddied by various interests, ranging from the federal government to states to tribes themselves.

But one thing is certain: Whatever definition of sovereignty is applied in debate, tribes are gaining more recognition as independent governments that must be dealt with on the same diplomatic, economic, and political terms as states—even as nations.

This is happening because tribes are gaining political influence by becoming wealthier than they have ever been, thanks to new revenue sources from gaming, the exploitation of natural resources on their trust lands, and legal settlements.

WHAT IS THE RELATIONSHIP BETWEEN STATE GOVERNMENTS AND TRIBAL GOVERNMENTS?

While tribes are gaining at the federal level in terms of their definition of sovereignty, much work remains to be done at the state level. For example, states may tax non-Indian businesses that operate on Indian lands. Some tribes that want to promote economic development find that they must hold back and not impose a tribal tax on those businesses, in order to prevent dual taxation from hindering growth.

Generally, however, Indian land is exempt from state laws, unless a federal law says otherwise, according to an opinion of the U.S. Supreme Court. Similarly,

Two Rivers Casino,
Spokane Reservation, Washington

crimes committed by American Indians on reservations are prosecuted either by tribal authorities or by the federal government. If a non-Indian commits a crime on an Indian reservation, however, the matter may be referred to the nearest appropriate court off the reservation for prosecution.

WHY CAN RESERVATIONS HAVE GAMBLING IF THE STATES THEY ARE IN DON'T ALLOW IT?

Because tribes are not under state jurisdiction, state laws banning or restricting casino-style gaming cannot apply to Indian lands. The Supreme Court has held in a number of cases that states cannot control or restrict tribal activities.

Those court opinions helped pave the way for the Indian Gaming Regulatory Act of 1988, which gave tribes the right to conduct "traditional" Indian gaming such as bingo, pull tabs, lotto, punch boards, tip jars, and certain card games on tribal land without state interference. However, the act requires a state and a tribe to form a compact, or agreement, for casino-style gaming such as cards or slot machines. Today there are about 145 tribal-state gaming compacts. In some cases, states benefit by receiving a small percentage of casino revenues. In other cases, the states will only agree to compacts that limit the size of the gaming operation or its proximity to urban areas. Nearly 130 tribes in 29 states are involved in some kind of casino-style gaming enterprise.

1978

Congress passes the American Indian Religious Freedom Act requiring federal agencies to analyze the impact of federal development on American Indian sacred sites and essentially granting to American Indians the equivalent of the First Amendment right to free exercise of religion.

1988

Congress enacts the Indian Gaming Regulatory Act (25 U.S.C. 2701), allowing gaming on reservations. In its broadest sense, the act reaffirms that tribes have the right to regulate gaming on their own lands, so long as the type of gaming is not expressly prohibited by the state where the Indian lands on which the gaming operation are situated. One caveat is casino-style (Class III) gaming, such as slots, which is allowed only as long as the tribe and the state in which their operation resides negotiate a regulatory compact. While states obtain some control over Indian gaming in this way, the federal government still shares in overseeing and tribes maintain control over most other types of gaming. Less than half have casino-style gaming operations, according to the National Indian Gaming Association.

Since states do not supervise gaming, Congress established the National Indian Gaming Commission to develop regulations for Indian gaming. The commission has overseen exponential growth in this arena. The year after the act passed in 1988, tribes with gaming compacts earned an aggregate gross annual revenue of $100 million from casino-style gaming. Just over ten years later, in 2000, the commission reported that the Indian gaming industry, as a whole, had $10.6 billion in gross revenues. These monies have funded new police and fire support for tribes, provided educational opportunities and jobs, and allowed tribal governments to provide new housing, plumbing, and electricity to members who live on the reservation.

HOW DO TRIBAL GOVERNMENTS WORK?

Today's modern tribal governments often have constitutions modeled after the U.S. Constitution. They have their own laws, courts, police, and public safety systems. Their governments include elected and appointed leaders, or representatives of the people, who make policy and negotiate with state and federal governments on behalf of the tribe.

Traditional forms of rule-making and decision-making operate alongside the modern tribal governments. For example, councils of elders, religious leaders, or dominant clans often must be consulted before new tribal policy moves forward.

LOVINIA MERSON AND SABRINA NOMEE, COEUR D'ALENE
Coeur d'Alene Reservation, Idaho

The introduction of modern governance modeled after non-Indian systems, while designed to provide economic and political empowerment, also sets the stage for cultural and political clashes. Today, it is not uncommon to hear about disputes between "traditionalists" and "modernists." And, the tribal council system of governance can sometimes work in direct opposition to a traditional form of decision-making. Phillip Reyna, a member of the Taos Pueblo, three hours drive north of Albuquerque, points out, for example, that the council is comprised entirely of men. Yet the Pueblo peoples have traditionally included women in important matters, from property ownership to crucial decision-making. Other tribes have similarly faced dilemmas of trying to decide whether to apply traditional or modern versions of governance and justice.

This has led to some unique and innovative results in recent years. One example is the Navajo Peacemaker Division, in which the traditional way of bringing entire families together to resolve a dispute is emphasized, rather than reliance on an adversarial relationship between plaintiff and defendant, as in the U.S. judicial system. The peacemaker is someone who facilitates

KARRIE PHILLIPS, NAVAJO
Student, member of the Shiprock boys and girls boxing team, Shiprock, New Mexico

a meeting with feuding parties. The peacemaker's goal is to resolve an issue to regain harmony in the traditional Navajo sense of balance. As for the parties in dispute, they must control themselves and be willing to listen and respect what the other party says. A dispute over ownership of a truck, for example, will bring two Navajo families to the table. The mission of the peacemaker is to ask, "Why is this dispute happening over property?"

"Navajos believe that there is an inner spirit to property," says Al Dennison, coordinator of the Peacemaker system. "They also believe that spoken words are powerful, so powerful that they inflict damage. So people must speak with respect toward each other and of property."

In 1993, the Tlingits also reverted to a traditional form of justice to discipline two teen-age members of the tribe who had committed a robbery that otherwise would have resulted in jail time. The Tlingits banished the young men from their home in Everett, Washington, to a remote Alaskan island, where they were forced to live for several months with no contact with the outside world. In this way, the traditional concepts of isolation leading to reflection and reform were allowed to carry themselves out.

1990

Congress passes Public Law 101-644 (1990) making it a crime for non-Indians to claim that their artwork is the "authentic" work of an American Indian.

DONALD KING, MARK PETTY, DAVID HICKMAN,
MISSISSIPPI CHOCTAW
Philadelphia, Mississippi

HOW DO TRIBES WORK TOGETHER?

Historically, American Indians who did not share the same cultural views were not unified politically. For example, from the 1700s into the early 1800s, some tribes would side with the French, others with the British or the United States, as Anglo-Europeans fought over the land and natural resources.

Today, groups such as the National Congress of American Indians (NCAI), All Indian Pueblo Council, intertribal councils in many states, and other special-interest groups coalesce around economic, political, and cultural issues. Other groups are more tightly focused. Consider the following examples: the Democratic Party's Native American Caucus in California, Intertribal Bison Cooperative, Intertribal Timber Council, Indigenous Environmental Network, Indigenous Women's Reproductive Rights, Faraway Cherokee Association of Memphis, InterTribal Technology Network, and more.

American Indian leaders disagree on just how effective these groups are. For example, the NCAI, considered one of the largest political coordinating bodies of tribes in the United States, is filled with raucous dissent. Many tribal leaders have called for its abolishment yet simultaneously seek out the unified support of member tribes. In many ways, that's the Indian way—free speech and dissent rule.

1991

In *Oregon v. Smith*, the U.S. Supreme Court essentially rules that First Amendment protections of American Indians are not expressly guaranteed if the practice violates a state law. In this case, the violation was using peyote as a sacrament in the Native American Church, even though Oregon had outlawed the use of peyote in any form.

DANIEL CONNOR AND JOHN ROBINSON,
LEECH LAKE BAND OF OJIBWE
Leech Lake Reservation, Cass Lake, Minnesota

There are things that pull tribes together, however. They are money, natural resources, and the right to self-govern.

"Gaming is bringing tribes together," said Mary Thomas, a former governor of the 6,000-member Gila River Indian Community, 30 miles southeast of Phoenix, Arizona. "The only thing that's terrible is that some of us remember history; we want to be rebellious at a time when cohesiveness is needed."

Tribes have a difficult time trusting each other. In the twenty-first century, they are seeking to heal centuries of political divisions. These divisions were created or worsened by the sudden and sometimes forced introduction of European cultures over the last 500 years. Thomas remembers the oral stories handed down from the elders. They tell of a time when her tribe and neighboring tribes in the Southwest sought harmony, even if once in a while they raided each other's camps. Balance was the rule, and an equal amount of give and take prevailed.

1993

The Religious Freedoms Restoration Act clarifies the *Oregon v. Smith* case to ensure that American Indians and other groups, such as the Amish, receive First Amendment religious protections.

* * * * *

Today, tribes, armed with economic empowerment and better-educated members, are finding sophisticated ways to use the traditions of the elders to bring balance and, with it, power in the complex international societies of the twenty-first century. Their new economic power also has given them new lobbying powers to influence political platforms benefiting tribes.

Tribes are shaping their own version of sovereignty in this millennium. Once again, they are becoming sovereign nations.

CORAZON LAFERN NOYOLA, SPOKANE/COLVILLE
Spokane Reservation, Washington